COLOR THE WORLD

ROUGH
GUIDES

INTRODUCTION

Travel broadens the mind while coloring calms and nourishes it. Combining the two, the designs on these pages transport you to some of the world's most spectacular sights, from the industrial artistry of Paris's Eiffel Tower to the centuries-old carvings of Angkor in Cambodia.

Fill in as much or as little of each pattern as you like. We recommend using colored pencils for the best effect but feel free to get creative. Break the rules. Go psychedelic! Whatever your approach, explore, be adventurous, and lose yourself in the beautiful patterns of this book.

LOCATION MAP

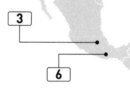

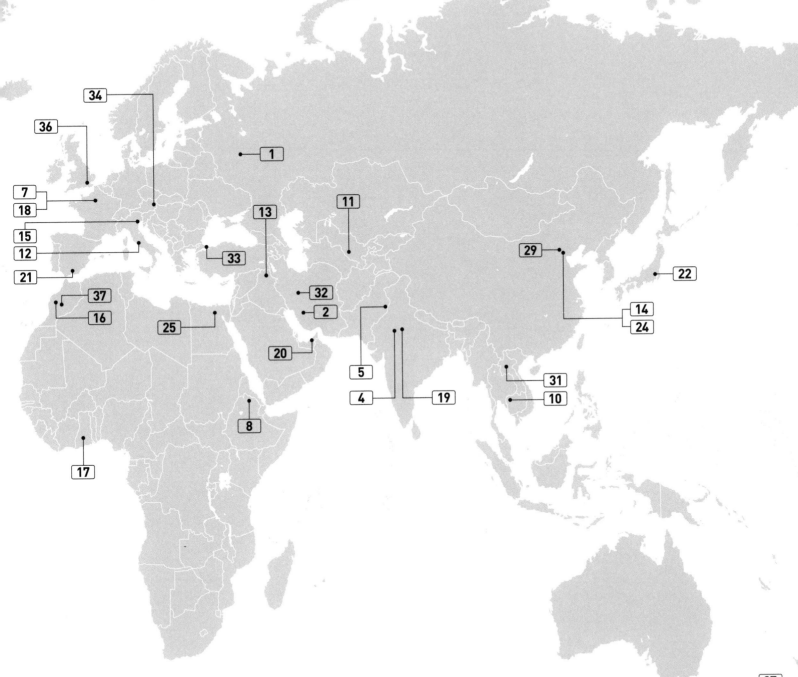

1

RUSSIA

The onion domes of St. Basil's Cathedral, Moscow

2

IRAN
The dazzling ceiling of Nasīr al-Mulk Mosque, Shiraz

3

MEXICO

An Aztec calendar stone discovered beneath the Zócalo, Mexico City's main square

4

INDIA
The peacock gate at the City Palace, Jaipur

5

PAKISTAN

The ceiling at the seventeenth-century Wazir Khan Mosque, Lahore

6

MEXICO
A Day of the Dead festival altar, Oaxaca

7

FRANCE
The Eiffel Tower, Paris

8

ETHIOPIA
Intricately woven baskets, Aksum

9

USA
The iconic Brooklyn Bridge, New York City

10

CAMBODIA
A decorative figure carved on a temple at Angkor

11

UZBEKISTAN
Ceiling fresco at Baha-ud-Din Naqshband Mausoleum, Bukhara

12

ITALY

The Colosseum, Rome's ancient gladiatorial arena

13
IRAQ

The ornate ceiling at the Jalil Khayat Mosque, Erbil

14

CHINA
Patriotic figurines at Panjiayuan Antique Market, Beijing

15

ITALY
A gondola on the Grand Canal, Venice

16

MOROCCO
Zellij tilework at Ben Youssef Medersa, a koranic school in Marrakesh

17

GHANA
Beautifully woven Kente cloth, Ashanti

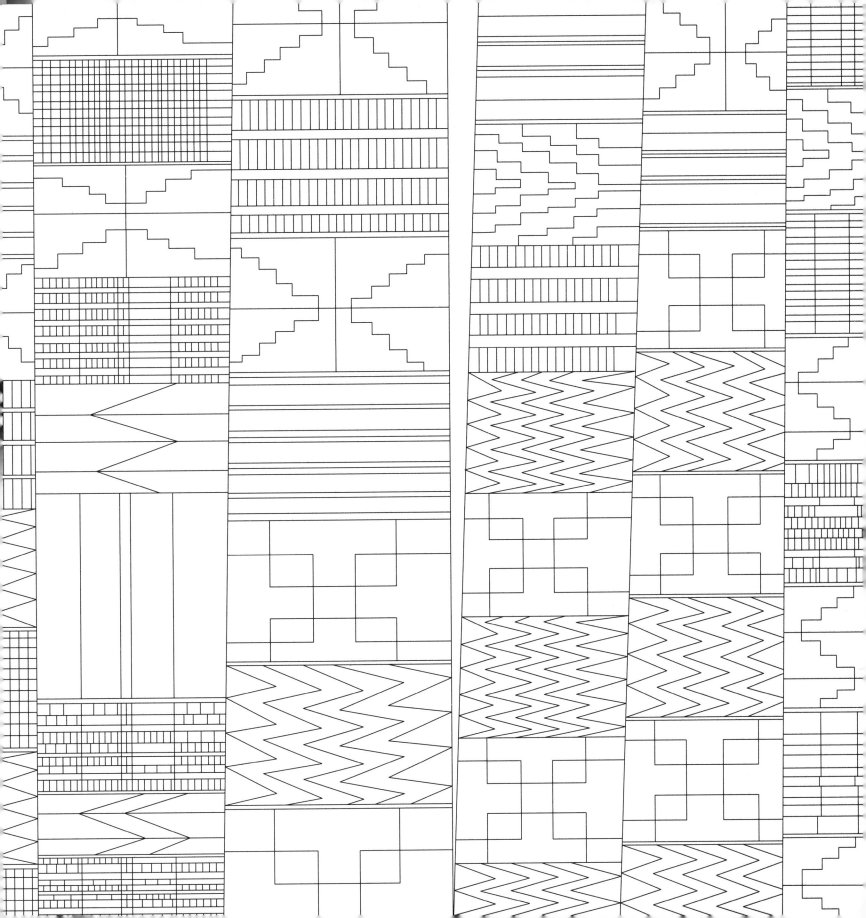

18

FRANCE
Rose window at the Sacré-Coeur basilica in Montmartre, Paris

19

INDIA
The opulent Taj Mahal mausoleum in Agra

20

ABU DHABI
Ceiling decoration at the Sheikh Zayed Grand Mosque

21

SPAIN
The Court of the Lions at the Alhambra, Granada

22

JAPAN

The bold neon lights of Tokyo

23

USA
The United States Capitol building, Washington, DC

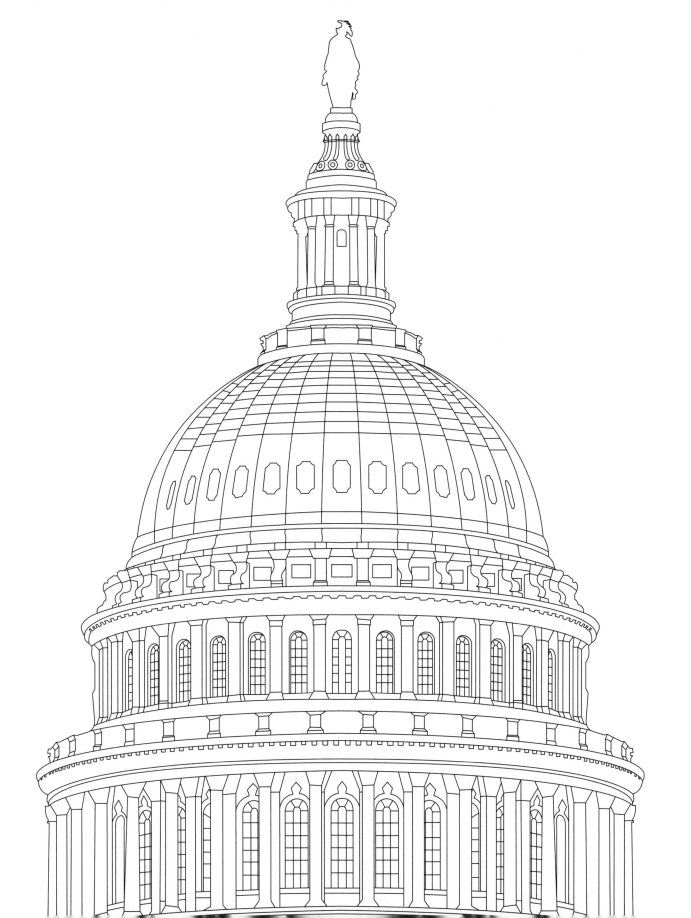

24

CHINA

The Palace Museum in the Forbidden City, Beijing

25

EGYPT

Gold burial mask of Tutankhamun at the Egyptian Museum, Cairo

26

CANADA

First Nations totem poles in Stanley Park, Vancouver

27

NEW ZEALAND
Maori carving from Ohinemutu village beside Lake Rotorua, North Island

28

TRINIDAD AND TOBAGO
Stilt walkers at Kiddies Carnival, Port of Spain, Trinidad

29

CHINA
The magnificent Great Wall of China

30

PERU
Machu Picchu, the ancient Inca citadel high in the Andes mountains

31

LAOS

Dolls on sale at a tribal market in Luang Prabang

32

IRAN
The ceiling dome of Sheikh Lotfollah Mosque, Isfahan

33

TURKEY

Decorative tiles from Istanbul's Topkapı Palace

34

AUSTRIA

The patterned roof of St. Stephen's Cathedral, Vienna

35

PUERTO RICO
A masked performer at Carnaval de Ponce

36

ENGLAND
Big Ben, the clocktower at London's Houses of Parliament

37

MOROCCO
Aït Benhaddou, a fortified town at the gateway to the Sahara

Senior editor Ros Walford
US Senior editor Shannon Beatty
Editorial assistant Freya Godfrey
Designer Priyanka Thakur, Vinita Venugopal
Senior cartographer Subhashree Bharati
Illustrators Hansa Babra, Bharti Karakoti, Arushi Kulkarni, Rahul Kumar, Bhavika Mathur, Arun Pottirayl, Ivy Roy Sengupta, Ankita Sharma, Priyanka Thakur, Tara Upadhyay, Vinita Venugopal, Richa Verma
Cover design Priyanka Thakur, Sarah Vance
Senior pre-press designer Dan May
Picture research Michelle Bhatia, Rituraj Singh
Senior producer Stephanie McConnell
Managing editor Andy Turner
Publisher Keith Drew
Publishing director Georgina Dee

Publishing information
Distributed by Penguin Random House
Penguin Books Ltd, 80 Strand, London WC2R 0RL
Penguin Group (USA), 345 Hudson Street, NY 10014, USA
Penguin Group (Australia), 250 Camberwell Road, Camberwell, Victoria 3124, Australia
Penguin Group (NZ), 67 Apollo Drive, Mairangi Bay, Auckland 1310, New Zealand
Penguin Group (South Africa), Block D, Rosebank Office Park, 181 Jan Smuts Avenue, Parktown North, Gauteng, South Africa 2193
Rough Guides is represented in Canada by DK Canada, 320 Front Street West, Suite 1400, Toronto, Ontario M5V 3B6

This first American edition published in July 2016 by
Rough Guides Ltd, 80 Strand, London WC2R 0RL

© Rough Guides 2016
A Penguin Random House Company

Printed and bound in China

16 17 18 19 10 9 8 7 6 5 4 3 2 1

A catalogue record for this book is available from the British Library

ISBN: 978-0-2412-8955-6

001–300149–Sep/16

The publishers and authors have done their best to ensure the accuracy of all the information in this book.

For more travel information, visit **roughguides.com**

Picture credits

The publisher would like to thank the following for their kind permission to reproduce their photographs:
(Key: a-above; b-below/bottom; c-center; f-far; l-left; r-right; t-top)

Numbers refer to the numbers on the main coloring pages.